IT'S THAT TIME OF YEAR!

Diwali

IS HERE!

BY VANESSA KAPADIA

It's That Time of Year! Diwali is Here!
A Fun Way to Teach Your Child About the Significance of the Days of Diwali
Book 1 of the It's That Time of Year Series.
Copyright © 2021 by Vanessa Kapadia

ISBN
978-0-6454876-4-0 (Hardcover)
978-0-6454876-3-3 (Paperback)
978-0-6454876-5-7 (eBook)

DEDICATION

For my beautiful son, Nayan:

May your light always shine
bright like the diyas of Diwali.

ACKNOWLEDGEMENTS

I would like to thank my wonderful
family for always supporting me in
all my endeavours throughout my
life, including creating this book.

Once a year, there are five days and nights

where my house and garden are filled with beautiful lights.

On those nights, we fold our hands and pray that the light from the night will stay bright for all the days.

It's that time of year!

On the 1st day, we worship Goddess Lakshmi, the goddess of wealth and prosperity.

Today is a good day to buy silver and gold. We also clean what we have, to return to new what was once old.

Dhanteras

How many diyas can you see?

On the 2nd day,
the whole family wakes up early and bathes,
to keep laziness and evil away.

We offer sweet, salty and spicy treats to Lord
Hanuman with a humble request;
that in the coming year we remain blessed.

Kali Chaudas

How many diyas can you see?

On the 3rd night, we do the Ganesh and Lakshmi Pujan.

We pray to them for an abundance of health, wealth, happiness, and protection.

We welcome the Goddess Lakshmi
by lighting diyas filled with ghee.

They are placed on the floor,
at all the doors.

We make our home nice and bright,
because Lakshmi loves to stay where there is light.

Diwali

How many diyas can you see?

The 4th day brings great cheer,
because it's the start of the new year!

We dress in new clothes, light sparklers, dance, and sing,
and look forward to what the coming year will bring.

Navu Varsh

How many diyas can you see?

The 5th and final day is where sisters are visited by their brothers.

They share food and sweets and wish the best for each other.

Bhai Beej

How many diyas can you see?

During Diwali, my family makes yummy

sweets that my friends and I love to eat.

My family makes lovely artwork called

Rangoli, where each picture helps tell a story.

Diwali is such a special festival!

Stick a picture of you
on Diwali here.

What part do you love best of all?

Made in the USA
Las Vegas, NV
19 October 2023

79337013R00017